# Not Bobby

## A Play

## N. J. Warburton

A Samuel French Acting Edition

SAMUELFRENCH-LONDON.CO.UK
SAMUELFRENCH.COM

Copyright © 1992 by N. J. Warburton
All Rights Reserved

NOT BOBBY is fully protected under the copyright laws of the British Commonwealth, including Canada, the United States of America, and all other countries of the Copyright Union. All rights, including professional and amateur stage productions, recitation, lecturing, public reading, motion picture, radio broadcasting, television and the rights of translation into foreign languages are strictly reserved.

ISBN 978-0-573-12179-1

www.samuelfrench-london.co.uk

www.samuelfrench.com

---

### FOR AMATEUR PRODUCTION ENQUIRIES

#### UNITED KINGDOM AND WORLD EXCLUDING NORTH AMERICA

plays@SamuelFrench-London.co.uk

020 7255 4302/01

Each title is subject to availability from Samuel French,

depending upon country of performance.

---

CAUTION: Professional and amateur producers are hereby warned that NOT BOBBY is subject to a licensing fee. Publication of this play does not imply availability for performance. Both amateurs and professionals considering a production are strongly advised to apply to the appropriate agent before starting rehearsals, advertising, or booking a theatre. A licensing fee must be paid whether the title is presented for charity or gain and whether or not admission is charged.

The professional rights in this play are controlled by David Higham Associates Ltd, 7th Floor, Waverley House, 7–12 Noel Street, London W1F 8GQ.

No one shall make any changes in this title for the purpose of production. No part of this book may be reproduced, stored in a retrieval system, or transmitted in any form, by any means, now known or yet to be invented, including mechanical, electronic, photocopying, recording, videotaping, or otherwise, without the prior written permission of the publisher. No one shall upload this title, or part of this title, to any social media websites.

The right of N. J. Warburton to be identified as author of this work has been asserted by him in accordance with Section 77 of the Copyright, Designs and Patents Act 1988

# NOT BOBBY

First performed at the Cambridge Drama Centre on the 19th August, 1991, with the following cast of characters:

| | |
|---|---|
| **Frank** | Jonathan Broughton |
| **Pam** | Mavis Perkins |
| **Ms Vincent/ Sophie/ Miss Bradfield** | Margaret McCarthy |

Production and stage management by Lynda Cliff, Katy Lown and Jenni Sinclair

The action takes place in the house of Frank and his mother, Pam

Time—the present

## CHARACTERS

**Frank Gideon**
**Pam Gideon**, his mother
**Ms Vincent**
**Sophie**
**Miss Bradfield**

Ms Vincent, Sophie and Miss Bradfield can be played by the same actress

# NOT BOBBY

*A rabbit cage is at the front of the stage, facing us. There are sounds of movement from within*

*The Lights come up to discover Frank and Pam seated. Frank is leafing through a newspaper, becoming more frantic as he fails to find what he's looking for. Pam reads a book*

**Frank** Is this it?
**Pam** Hmm?
**Frank** I said, is this it?
**Pam** (*looking up*) What?
**Frank** The paper. Is this all there is?
**Pam** The supplements, you mean?
**Frank** No. I've got the supplements. The main paper, I mean. There's pages missing.
**Pam** Oh dear. You ought to complain.
**Frank** It's not the paper's fault, Mother. There's pages been taken out.
**Pam** Ah.
**Frank** Ah? You know about it, do you? I mean, you sound as if you know about it.
**Pam** I might. It could be the page I took out.

**Frank** You took a page out? From today's paper?
**Pam** I thought it was yesterday's, Frank. I haven't seen today's...
**Frank** Well it was yesterday's but I'm reading it today. I always read it the day after.
**Pam** Do you?
**Frank** I thought you knew that.
**Pam** Did I?
**Frank** I thought so. On a Monday. Monday's papers include the bits of Sunday's which I don't have time to read.
**Pam** I see. (*Beat*) I could help, if you like.
**Frank** What?
**Pam** I could read some for you. Then you might get them all done in the day.
**Frank** It's not because I'm slow, Mother. It's because there's so much. (*Pause*) So what did you want it for?
**Pam** Hmm?
**Frank** A page from the paper. What was it for?
**Pam** Oh. I put a fresh page in the rabbit's cage. On a Monday. I always do that. I thought you knew.
**Frank** Always? We've only had the rabbit a fortnight.
**Pam** Well, I've only done it twice, then.
**Frank** I'm not sure that was wise.
**Pam** I didn't really look. I mean, you can't tell a paper's been read just by looking at it...
**Frank** I mean put newspaper in a rabbit's cage.
**Pam** What?
**Frank** I read it somewhere. Something to do with the ink.
**Pam** The ink?
**Frank** Yes. It could poison them.
**Pam** Oh, the poor little thing.
**Frank** He hasn't shown any signs, has he?
**Pam** No. He never touches it as far as I can tell. Well, only with his feet. Is that why you asked?

**Frank** What?
**Pam** About the missing page. Is that what you thought I'd done with it?
**Frank** No. No, no. It was the crossword. I hadn't finished it.
**Pam** Oh. (*Beat*) Do you, though? I mean, do you finish it?
**Frank** Well, no. Not normally. It's just that yesterday I did.
**Pam** (*impressed*) Oh.
**Frank** Well, nearly did. Just two clues to go. I've been thinking about them, on and off, all day in the office.
**Pam** Slack, is it?
**Frank** What?
**Pam** Not very busy.
**Frank** It's quite busy enough. But they don't own my mind, Mother. I can check through development proposals *and* think about crossword clues at the same time.
**Pam** And what does Mr Lennox think about that?
**Frank** I didn't tell Mr Lennox.
**Pam** You don't have to *tell* Mr Lennox things. (*Beat*) So you worked it out, then?
**Frank** Ah. That's the funny thing. I stopped thinking about the clues and suddenly I got one. You know how it is.
**Pam** Out of the blue.
**Frank** Yes. So I thought I'd fill it in.
**Pam** Oh. Pity.
**Frank** Pity?
**Pam** Well, you can't now, can you?
**Frank** No. (*Beat*) Has it been out there long? I mean, if he's been asleep or something...
**Pam** What?
**Frank** It might be all right.
**Pam** I wouldn't fancy it.
**Frank** No but you said yourself he's a clean animal and if it's only just been put out there. Has it?

**Pam**  About an hour or so.
**Frank**  (*getting up*) Oh well then...
**Pam**  Frank!
**Frank**  Yes but only an hour, Mother...
**Pam**  An hour's long enough. For a rabbit. I don't want you bringing it back in here, Frank. I wouldn't let Daddy do a thing like that...
**Frank**  Daddy never had a rabbit.
**Pam**  And there's no need for smart answers. You're not in the office now.
**Frank**  I'll only look. I don't plan to bring it in.

*Pam doesn't respond*

I'm only interested in the crossword. And only one bit of that. I could tear it off. That bit might be all right.

*Still no response*

I'm just saying. Rabbit droppings, well, it's not like dogs, is it? I mean...
**Pam**  Just go if you're going. You'll have me retching in a minute.

*Frank gets up and peers into the cage. He opens it and slides a sheet of newspaper out. He looks at it, holds it up to the lights and looks back in the cage. Pam attempts to read but her attention keeps wandering to Frank*

Frank.
**Frank**  Yes?
**Pam**  Have you finshed or what?

*Frank returns, holding the sheet of newspaper before him*

**Frank** Mother...
**Pam** Not in here!
**Frank** There's something wrong here...
**Pam** For God's sake. I give Dr Heron his tea in here.
**Frank** It's this crossword, Mother.
**Pam** (*averting her eyes*) I know it's the crossword.
**Frank** You didn't finish it before you put it in the cage, did you?
**Pam** Of course I didn't.
**Frank** You'd've said, wouldn't you? Knowing I was so close.
**Pam** I didn't finish it, Frank.
**Frank** No. (*Beat*) Someone else has, then.
**Pam** Oh, good. Will you take it out now? Please.
**Frank** I mean, who could have? (*He has a sudden thought*) Rita didn't come round, did she?
**Pam** No. Look, Frank...
**Frank** She didn't finish it while your back was turned, did she? D'you think?
**Pam** She hasn't been round.
**Frank** So what's happened?
**Pam** It's a crossword, Frank. What does it matter?
**Frank** I mean, what's happened here? Someone broke in, finished the crossword, broke out again? You're not telling me it was that, I hope?
**Pam** Of course not...
**Frank** Because I wouldn't believe it.
**Pam** You did it yourself.
**Frank** What?
**Pam** You must've finished it without realizing.
**Frank** Don't be daft.
**Pam** You could've done. Daddy always used to say...
**Frank** And we don't want that particular record, thank you.
**Pam** What?

**Frank** Daddy always used to say.
**Pam** Well he did..
**Frank** I know! I spent half my life listening to him say it, and the other half listening to you repeat it. Daddy had nothing to say about this, Mother. Believe me. (*Pause*) That pencil. The one we use for shopping lists.
**Pam** The thick one?
**Frank** That smudges, yes. Where is it?
**Pam** Why?

*Frank produces the pencil and holds it up*

**Frank** It was in the cage.
**Pam** Ah. Yes, it could've been.
**Frank** Could've been? It was.
**Pam** I mean, I used it this afternoon, to poke the carrot through the wire.
**Frank** You should open the door.
**Pam** I don't like to. I'm not quite used to him yet.
**Frank** Well, he was your idea.
**Pam** He wasn't. You suggested him.
**Frank** Only because you said you always wanted a rabbit.
**Pam** Did I?
**Frank** Of course you did. You said Daddy would never allow you to have one and...
**Pam** Yes, well, I didn't know you'd go out and buy one, did I?
**Frank** What did you expect me to go out and buy? (*Beat*) So you poked the carrot in, using a pencil?
**Pam** Yes. And he gave a little gallop.
**Frank** Yes?
**Pam** And it, well, startled me and I dropped the pencil.
**Frank** Didn't you get it back?
**Pam** No. I told you, I'm not used to him yet.

**Frank** But you only had to slide the door open.
**Pam** Look, I dropped a pencil in the rabbit's cage, Frank. What do you want? Legal proceedings?
**Frank** Don't be silly. All I'm saying is this: you put the crossword down for him...
**Pam** I put the newspaper down, Frank. I didn't know it was the crossword.
**Frank** But it was. And then you dropped the pencil in.
**Pam** Yes?
**Frank** And now the crossword's finished. And he's looking pleased with himself.

*The Lights fade*

*The Lights come up. Ms Vincent is in one of the chairs drinking tea*

**Vincent** Ah, yes. Very good. (*To Pam*) I'm not just saying that, Mrs Gideon. I do mean it. You can go a long way these days before you come across a lady prepared to do without the convenience of a bag. (*She drinks*) No, it's what I call "outside the circle of normal things". I grant you that. We can't proceed until we bring the matter within that circle, so to say. This is the crux. To put it bluntly, what are we going to do about it?
**Frank** Well, we have done something.
**Vincent** Have you?
**Frank** Yes. We've got in touch with you.
**Vincent** Yes, I see.
**Pam** And we're wondering what you intend to do about it.
**Vincent** Of course. Well at this stage, I'd like to do little more than suggest that... he can no longer be considered as... a mere rabbit.
**Pam** Can't he?

**Vincent** Not now. He's completed a crossword puzzle.
**Frank** Two clues, though. I did the rest.
**Vincent** Of course. But that's not quite such a phenomenon, is it?
**Pam** He's never managed it before.
**Vincent** Perhaps not, but we're still inclined to be more impressed by the rabbit. I hope you don't think that's unfair.
**Frank** Oh no.
**Vincent** Good. If we assume that what happened the other evening was not a coincidence along the lines of monkeys with typewriters...
**Pam** Monkeys?
**Vincent** Tapping out the works of Shakespeare. At random. If we assume there's more to it than that, we must conclude that a) the rabbit read the clues, and b) that he actually worked them out and wrote in the answers.
**Frank** He did. I can't see what else could've happened.
**Vincent** Quite. Quite. Which brings us back to the original problem. Where do we go from here?
**Pam** Is it a problem, though?
**Vincent** It is now, yes. Once you picked up that phone and told us about the little fellow, well, it became impossible for us to ignore him. Does he have a name, by the way?
**Pam** We haven't decided, have we, Frank?
**Frank** Not really.
**Pam** Although I always...
**Vincent** Yes?
**Pam** I always think of him as Bobby.
**Frank** Bobby? You never said.
**Pam** No, I know. I was trying it out. To myself. I didn't want to force your hand.
**Vincent** Bobby seems adequate to me.
**Frank** Well... I don't know...

**Vincent** (*writing it down*) Let's stick with Bobby for the time being, shall we? I just need to call him something.
**Pam** Do you? Why?
**Vincent** This is what I'm leading up to, Mrs Gideon. I've had a lengthy meeting with the Chief Education Officer and, after a considerable amount of wrangling, we've agreed that this is something of a special case. It's a matter of classification, really.
**Frank** Is it?
**Vincent** Yes. Young Bobby is a thinking, communicating being, you see.
**Frank** He doesn't speak, Ms Vincent.
**Vincent** No, I realize that. But he writes. So he is, at least as far as the Department is concerned, less of a pet and more of a... a responsibility.
**Frank** So, what are you getting at?
**Vincent** (*beat*) We see Bobby as a child.
**Pam** A child?
**Vincent** A child. This is how he has now been classified. On the strength of the crossword.
**Frank** You don't mean a child rabbit? You mean...
**Vincent** We mean what you probably think we mean, Mr Gideon.
**Frank** I see.
**Vincent** It can't be that much of a surprise to you. After all, you did contact the Local Education Authority so you probably had children in the back of your mind.
**Pam** We contacted the zoo, too, didn't we, Frank?
**Frank** But they weren't interested.
**Vincent** Our experts calculate that he must have a reading age of eight plus. We can't be more precise than that because there are certain difficulties over his chronological age. However, we had to classify him as either a child, which, in some superficial

respects, he clearly is not, or as a pet, which, in a more drastic way, he is not either. So, given that he must be one or the other, it has been decided that he is the former.

**Pam** A child?

**Vincent** Yes.

**Frank** I see.

**Vincent** I'm glad you do, Mr Gideon, because at the moment Bobby exhibits a certain potential which, we feel, is not being challenged.

**Pam** Yes, but...

**Vincent** Please, don't be offended. We're sure that he's happy here at home. But that's not the point.

**Frank** Well, what is the point?

**Vincent** A child at that level should be stretched more.

**Pam** Stretched?

**Vincent** There are attainment targets which should be set for him.

**Frank** At school, you mean?

**Vincent** Probably.

**Frank** But he's a rabbit.

**Vincent** Only up to a point, Mr Gideon. (*Beat*) You can educate him yourselves, of course.

**Pam** We can?

**Frank** Here at home?

**Vincent** Oh, yes. The law allows for that. As long as you satisfy us that he will be exposed to the full breadth of the National Curriculum.

**Frank** I'm not sure we could do that. What do you think, Mother?

**Pam** Oh, no. I couldn't see myself doing that.

**Vincent** Alternatively, there is the private sector, which, at least as far the National Curriculum is concerned, is exempt.

**Frank** You mean Bobby could get away without doing it?

**Vincent** In a manner of speaking. The National Curriculum is

# Not Bobby

merely—how shall I put it?—a safeguard for children whose parents can't afford the cream.

**Frank**  So, we're talking about Eton or something, are we?

**Vincent**  Eton, possibly. Or any one of a number of establishments. A prep school in the first instance, probably. You haven't put Bobby's name down for a prep school, I suppose.

**Frank**  Well... no, we haven't...

**Vincent**  That's all right. Don't blame yourselves.

**Pam**  It's the expense...

**Vincent**  Of course. If it wasn't for the expense we'd all do it, wouldn't we?

**Frank**  I'm not saying we won't, Ms Vincent. Or that we can't. We just haven't gone into costings and things.

**Pam**  We'd want to do our best by him, wouldn't we, Frank?

**Frank**  Oh yes, and, I mean, Bobby's not very big, is he?

**Vincent**  Not very big?

**Frank**  They might offer a reduction...

**Vincent**  I doubt it. Not merely on size. Besides, in Bobby's case, the money may not be the only obstacle. I'm thinking more of the uniform.

**Pam**  Uniform?

**Vincent**  They're awfully keen on uniform and that may prove a little difficult here. You wouldn't get much "off the peg" for Bobby, as it were.

**Pam**  We could have something made up, in school colours.

**Vincent**  I'm sure you could. However, it would differ so greatly from the uniforms of the other children that, well, it would no longer be uniform in the true sense of the word, would it?

**Frank**  I suppose not.

**Pam**  So, it has to be a state school...

**Vincent**  That's probably the best place to start, yes.

**Pam**  Oh. Seems a shame.

**Frank**  You sent me to a state school...

**Pam** You went to Daddy's old school, Frank.

**Frank** Only because it was round the corner.

**Vincent** Well, there's something to be said for proximity, isn't there? Bobby may find it strange to begin with but children are resilient by nature. They adjust very quickly. And I'm here to help. If you have any questions or concerns...

**Frank** No, I don't think so. I can't think of anything, can you, Mother?

**Pam** I don't know. He seems so content with life, as he finds it at the moment.

**Frank** If it's the law, though.

**Pam** I just wonder if he isn't a bit young to be thinking of school. We didn't send Frank till he was five.

**Frank** That's a point. Don't they have to be five, Ms Vincent?

**Vincent** Five-ish, yes.

**Frank** Well Bobby's not yet one.

**Vincent** Ah. This proved to be something of a stumbling block for the Chief Education Office, too. If we wait till Bobby's rising five, though, we could find ourselves with a very mature little chap on our hands. Which would be rather silly. In rabbit terms he'd be quite old. More of a candidate for the Open University.

**Pam** You mean he could get a degree?

**Vincent** I think it's too soon to speculate about that.

**Pam** It would be nice to have a degree in the family, wouldn't it, Frank?

**Vincent** No, the point is, he may be intellectually ready for the greater challenge of a degree course at five but he'd lack the basic skills to cope with one. What we've done is come up with a sliding scale which gives a fairer reflection of Bobby's age. And that places him at about seven. A bright seven, as I said before, but it's probably best to put him in at the top infant range and see how he gets on.

*The Lights fade*

*Ms Vincent exits*

*When the Lights come up Frank is reading and Pam is taking some simple books, alphabet charts, etc. from a box and arranging them on the cage*

**Pam** (*opening one of the books*) Oh look, Bobby. *British Wildlife.* I wonder if you're in it... (*She thumbs through*) Yes. Here we are. The rabbit.

*She shows him but there is no response so she thumbs through some more*

And hedgehogs... and a fox... Bobby, don't turn your back; it's only a picture. Bobby? (*She steps back, slightly disgusted*) There was no need for that, was there? Is that a coincidence, do you think?
**Frank** What?
**Pam** What he did just then. Or did he do it on purpose?
**Frank** Why should he do it on purpose?
**Pam** I'm not sure, Frank. I was showing him this book and he took exception to one of the pictures. It could be a coincidence, I suppose.

*Frank gets up and crosses to Bobby*

**Frank** Bobby? What's all this about, eh?
**Pam** Don't snap at him, Frank. We don't know that he meant it...
**Frank** It's best to be on the safe side, though. (*To Bobby*) That's not a very pleasant form of protest, Bobby. We don't do that

kind of thing.
**Pam** Don't tell him that. You'll confuse him.
**Frank** Why?
**Pam** Well... he has to function, Frank...
**Frank** Oh, I see. (*To Bobby*) Look, Bobby, we don't do that kind of thing just to show we're annoyed, do we? Eh? What would Mr Lennox say if I went in on Monday morning and...
**Pam** Frank!
**Frank** What?
**Pam** I think that's quite enough. We don't want to make mountains out of molehills, do we?
**Frank** Oh. All right, Mother. I think he's got the message anyway.

*The doorbell sounds. They freeze*

**Pam** It's them.
**Frank** Yes. Look, you let them in, Mother. And knock up a bit of tea or something.
**Pam** Yes. Yes, that would be best.

*The bell sounds again*

*Pam looks anxiously at Frank and then exits*

*Frank attempts to smarten himself up. He tries to sit, nonchalantly and relaxed, but it doesn't come off*

*Sophie enters and watches*

*Frank notices her and jumps up*

**Frank** Oh. Er... do come in...

**Sophie** (*confidently*) I am in.
**Frank** Yes. Yes, of course. Take a seat, Mrs er...
**Sophie** Sophie. (*She sits, looking immediately nonchalant and relaxed*) Well, how are things?
**Frank** Oh, you know. Fine...
**Sophie** Settling in?
**Frank** We've always been here, actually. Well, I have. Mother used to live...
**Sophie** I meant Bobby. At school.
**Frank** Oh, yes. Of course. Bobby. Well, yes. You know. So far so...
**Sophie** Good, good. No problems, then?
**Frank** I don't think so.
**Sophie** Splendid. I can pass that on, then, can I?
**Frank** Sorry?
**Sophie** To the PTA. We like to know that people are, you know, satisfied with what's going on.
**Frank** Satisfied?
**Sophie** Yes. That's what I'm trying to ascertain. I want to fit your little worries and doubts into the broader picture.
**Frank** Oh, I see.
**Sophie** It can be a trial, can't it? Those awkward first few weeks.
**Frank** Can it?
**Sophie** They don't always adjust. Precious moments of education slip by and they just sit in the sandpit wondering what's hit them. Poor things.
**Frank** Though sand in itself, can be, well it can be...
**Sophie** What?
**Frank** You know: educational.
**Sophie** (*with a short laugh*) I can see you've already had Mr Hendry's pep talk for new parents, Frank. It is Frank, isn't it?
**Frank** Yes, that's right.
**Sophie** I shouldn't take too much notice of that.

**Frank** Really?

**Sophie** Think about it, Frank. Sand is educational? Creative? Can you explain to me how?

**Frank** Well, it's ... it's...

**Sophie** Of course you can't. It just doesn't tie up, does it? OK if you want them to work in Saudi Arabia or something but you can hardly know that at five, can you?

**Frank** No, I suppose not.

**Sophie** No. I'm afraid Mr Hendry and I have locked horns over the sand pit many times this year. He's a nice enough man, in his way, but when he flounders he tends to burble about sand and creativity. It's a way of deflecting argument.

**Frank** I see.

**Sophie** Mr Hendry is the head. He's in the business of selling what the school has to offer, I mean. Whereas I, well, I'm...

**Frank** In the business of satisfaction.

**Sophie** I'm in the business of quality control, you might say. Why don't you sit down, Frank?

**Frank** (*doing so*) Oh. Thanks.

**Sophie** Let me give you an example. Did you know that Bobby is on Greens?

**Frank** What?

**Sophie** At school. He's on Greens.

**Frank** Well, he's a vegetarian.

**Sophie** I mean, he's on the Green books. Green Book 3a, to be precise.

**Frank** Is he?

**Sophie** So Daisy tells me.

**Frank** Daisy?

**Sophie** My daughter. She's in the same class as Bobby.

**Frank** And she knows what book Bobby's on?

**Sophie** I encourage Daisy to tell me things like that. That sort of openness is necessary these days.

**Frank** Well, yes, of course...
**Sophie** The thing is, Frank, I think you and I could work together on this one. Quite closely. If that's all right with you.
**Frank** Quite closely?
**Sophie** Yes. I could, perhaps, hear him read.
**Frank** What, Bobby?
**Sophie** Yes. You see, Daisy's on Green 2c. Which is several books lower than Bobby...
**Frank** Really?
**Sophie** And I'm pretty sure Miss Bradfield's cocked this one up. After all, Bobby's just joined the school. He spends a fortnight in the sandpit and, miracle of miracles, he manages to leapfrog Daisy on to Green 3a. Does that sound right to you?
**Frank** Well...
**Sophie** You wouldn't think so if you could hear Daisy read at home. She reads fluently, Frank. With a rare fluency, in fact. You have to make her face up to it, of course, and that's where Miss Bradfield and I part company. Miss Bradfield sees her a tender flower. She has no idea what a tough little bitch Daisy can be when she wants to.
**Frank** I'm not sure I can help here, Mrs er...
**Sophie** Sophie.
**Frank** Sophie. I mean, what has this got to do with Bobby?
**Sophie** I explained that. I know what Daisy can do. Now I'd like to hear Bobby. For purposes of comparison. With my PTA hat on.
**Frank** Well, Bobby's very quiet, you see. He doesn't say much. I don't think it's possible...
**Sophie** You can trust me, Frank. It'll go no further than these four walls. Won't you let me press you?
**Frank** I'd like to help...
**Sophie** It would be such a help to Daisy. The poor girl worries herself sick about being on Green 2c. Look, we're just getting

to know each other. I don't want to hassle you. Think about it, OK?

**Frank** I'll think about it, of course.

**Sophie** Daisy would be so grateful. And so would I. (*She notices the cage*) Is this Bobby's?

**Frank** Yes. It's ... er...

**Sophie** I'm rather surprised. I won't allow Daisy to have pets.

**Frank** Pets?

**Sophie** They're a distraction. This was one of Mr Hendry's suggestions, was it?

**Frank** No. Bobby's always... I mean...

**Sophie** It's not really necessary. I take Daisy to safari parks. For biological purposes. The last time we went we saw lions mating. Daisy found it quite awe-inspiring.

**Frank** Really?

**Sophie** Yes. It was all very languid.

**Frank** I see.

**Sophie** So. Where is the little fellow?

**Frank** (*looking at the cage*) He's ... he's out at the moment.

**Sophie** At this hour?

**Frank** Yes. He's... gone to the pictures.

**Sophie** Gone to the pictures? Is that entirely appropriate? Who with?

**Frank** With Mother.

**Sophie** Your mother? (*Looking over her shoulder*) But I thought...

**Frank** Yes. No. Mother's in the kitchen.

**Sophie** So?

**Frank** With Rita. Who's someone else's mother. (*He laughs*) You know how it is.

**Sophie** It's all right. There's no need to be coy about it, Frank. Not these days.

**Frank** No, no. Rita lives next door. She's...

**Sophie** It's all right. Daisy's a love-child too. It's nothing to be ashamed of.

**Frank** (*floundering*) No, you don't understand. Bobby's not... he's not... (*He sees a piece of paper on the coffee table*) Ah. This is Bobby's. Something he wrote. If that's any help to you. (*He hands her the paper*)

**Sophie** Yes. Thank you. (*Turning it over*) Is this all?

**Frank** Well, it's a bit rough, of course...

**Sophie** Carrots?

**Frank** Yes.

**Sophie** With one 'r'?

**Frank** Is it?

**Sophie** Oh dear. This doesn't look like the work of someone on Green 3a to me.

**Frank** Doesn't it?

**Sophie** Daisy could knock this kind of thing into a cocked hat, Frank.

**Frank** Really?

**Sophie** (*standing*) And you've let him go to the pictures with your woman? If I were you I'd be straight up to the school at the first opportunity and slam this down on Hendry's desk.

**Frank** (*standing*) I see.

**Sophie** Most certainly. Perhaps I'll see you there.

**Frank** Will you?

**Sophie** Oh, I'll be there, Frank. I'll have a bone or two to pick with Miss Bradfield. First thing tomorrow morning.

*Sophie exits as Pam enters with a tray*

**Pam** Oh.

**Frank** She couldn't stay. Apparently.

**Pam** You didn't tell me it was her.

**Frank** I didn't know until she turned up. She... she seemed quite

nice.
**Pam** Really? That's not what I've heard in the butcher's.
**Frank** She's all right. She was here with her PTA hat on.
**Pam** (*putting the tray down*) PTA legs might be nearer the mark.
**Frank** For goodness sake, Mother.
**Pam** Funny, isn't it? You go out and buy a rabbit and before you know what's going on your son's closeted in the front room with a single parent.
**Frank** We were not closeted. And *I* bought Bobby, remember. (*Beat*) She doesn't think Bobby is up to scratch.
**Pam** Why?
**Frank** She was looking at that note. About carrots. I don't think she's twigged that he's a rabbit. All the same...
**Pam** What?
**Frank** Well, it was a bit of a scrawl.
**Pam** He conveys his meaning. We've always said that.
**Frank** I know but are we being too soft on him, Mother? That's what I'm wondering. He sits in there for ages doing nothing.
**Pam** Well, he could come out. I don't mind.
**Frank** He doesn't do anything if he does come out, though. He just sits on the carpet. Maybe we should push him a bit more.
**Pam** Push him?
**Frank** Extend him. Make him work a bit harder. He does the bare minimum for school when you think about it. He's going to fall behind if he's not careful.
**Pam** He's all right.
**Frank** He won't thank us for it, Mother. Not when it comes to exams and he finds he can't cope. He's going to wonder why we didn't insist.
**Pam** Oh Frank. He's too young to be worrying about exams.
**Frank** He's very far from too young. What about all that Seven Year Test business.
**Pam** What about it?

# Not Bobby

**Frank**  It was a fiasco. It took so long to administer that Bobby was a year too old by the time they'd worked out the results.
**Pam**  Rabbit years.
**Frank**  All the same, he was marked down for it. I'm not convinced he's putting his back into it like he should. (*Beat*) Take that letter he had to write.
**Pam**  What letter?
**Frank**  For school. Miss Bradfield sent the details home. He had to write a letter to a friend.
**Pam**  He did. He did write to a friend.
**Frank**  He wrote one word, Mother. I don't call one word a letter.
**Pam**  He hasn't got friends like the other children. He never brings anyone back to play, does he?
**Frank**  This is what I'm saying. He doesn't work and he doesn't play. He just sits there. I don't think it's normal.
**Pam**  If he hasn't got friends I don't see how he can write letters to them.
**Frank**  Yes but it was an exercise, wasn't it. It was to prepare him for later life.
**Pam**  (*to the cage*) Take no notice, Bobby. Your Aunty Pam knows you do your best.
**Frank**  A one word letter? That's his best?
**Pam**  It made sense though.
**Frank**  It was highly irregular.
**Pam**  I don't see why.
**Frank**  You don't see why? Tell me, then. Who was it for?
**Pam**  I told you, Bobby doesn't make friends...
**Frank**  So who was it for?
**Pam**  Fluff.
**Frank**  Fluff. The rabbit in the middle infants' class. Exactly. And what did it say?
**Pam**  Well...
**Frank**  It said "babies", Mother. "Babies". I think that's fairly

clear, don't you?

**Pam**  Fluff couldn't read it. Even if we'd passed it on.

**Frank**  Thank God for that. What kind of example is that to set the other children? And what kind of job is he going to get if he only writes letters of one word?

**Pam**  Job?

**Frank**  Oh, Mother. You can't keep turning your back on the problem. He's got to start thinking of the future.

**Pam**  Well I'd've thought he was thinking about the future...

**Frank**  I'm not talking about Fluff. I'm talking about employment. I'm talking about what he's going to find when he gets out into the market place.

**Pam**  I didn't think he'd have a job.

**Frank**  Why on earth not? (*Beat*) I had to get a job.

**Pam**  That's different...

**Frank**  Oh that's nice. It's different for Bobby. Yes, of course. Off you go to work, Frank, and don't come back here till you can start paying for your keep.

**Pam**  I never said that.

**Frank**  You did. Of course you did. You and Daddy both. But things are different now. Bobby doesn't have to get a job all of a sudden. Bobby can sit on his bum all day doing nothing...

**Pam**  Frank! Don't talk like that. Daddy and I did all we could for you.

**Frank**  You never talked about degrees when I was at school. I was pushed out to work at the first opportunity.

**Pam**  You wanted to go out to work...

**Frank**  How did you know? How could you possibly tell that?

**Pam**  You said you did.

**Frank**  Well, of course I did. Because I know that's what you wanted.

**Pam**  Didn't you?

**Frank**  No.

**Pam** Well, it's a bit late to bring it up now, Frank. You've been in that office for twelve years.
**Frank** You don't have to remind me.
**Pam** Daddy and I couldn't read minds, you know. If you wanted to do a degree you should've said...
**Frank** (*sighing*) There's no point in talking about it now...
**Pam** Yes there is. If you've been harbouring grudges all these years; if Daddy and I have been holding you back...
**Frank** I didn't say that.
**Pam** In all but actual words, Frank, I think you said exactly that. Never a thank you for the sacrifices we had to make, I notice.
**Frank** Sacrifices? Daddy never gave up a thing for me.
**Pam** Listen to me, Frank Gideon. It's time you faced a few home truths. You're turning into a very bitter boy. You can't blame Daddy for your own shortcomings.
**Frank** I'm not. I'm only...
**Pam** Don't wriggle out of it now. You've got me started, Frank, so you can just listen for a change. Daddy went round and begged Mr Lennox to take you on. Cap in hand. And that wasn't a thing Daddy liked to do. But he did it. For you. He put your feet on the ladder. And what happened? I'll tell you what happened. Lesley Banks, that's what happened. There's no need to roll your eyes. You had success on a plate, Frank, and you threw it away for the sake of... of a tart.
**Frank** That's right, bring Lesley Banks into it...
**Pam** You're the one who brought her into it, Frank. Into this house, without a word of warning...
**Frank** Mother, you make her sound like a stray. We were engaged, you know.
**Pam** Engaged?
**Frank** Practically.
**Pam** There was no party, Frank. No ring. No announcements.
**Frank** Yes and we all know why.

**Pam** Some of us knew that before she got her claws out.
**Frank** She never got her claws out...
**Pam** You should've talked to us, Frank. You're too secretive. You know what Daddy has always said.
**Frank** For God's sake. Not that!
**Pam** You need never be ashamed of your feelings.
**Frank** Daddy never had any feelings.
**Pam** You... slug! To turn on your own father like that!
**Frank** What about my feelings for Lesley? You taught me to be ashamed of them.

*The row has become quite fierce. A thumping sound from inside the cage brings about an abrupt pause*

   Now what?
**Pam** Bobby! Bobby, what's the matter?
**Frank** For goodness sake. What's got into him now?
**Pam** It's a message. He's left a message.
**Frank** Bobby! What did I just tell you?
**Pam** No, he's written a message. Look.

*Frank takes a piece of paper from the wires of the cage. The row has now subsided*

   What does it say?
**Frank** "Not Bobby".
**Pam** "Not Bobby"? Is that all?
**Frank** That's all. He's a bit terse, isn't he?
**Pam** I suppose so. He gets his meaning over, though.
**Frank** Not Bobby.
**Pam** Yes.
**Frank** I wasn't exactly happy about Bobby myself.
**Pam** About the name?

**Frank** Yes. I was thinking more of...
**Pam** What?
**Frank** I don't know. Neville?
**Pam** Neville?
**Frank** But he's been enrolled at the school as Bobby. I can't go back up there and say he's not Bobby anymore...
**Pam** But if a thing's worth doing, Frank...
**Frank** I'm not sure what they'll think of me if I do. And what happens if he doesn't like Neville? I can't keep going up there till we hit on something he likes.
**Pam** No. Perhaps not.
**Frank** Besides, no-one asked me if I wanted to be called Francis. I just had to get used to it.
**Pam** Don't you like it, then?
**Frank** I don't know. I never thought about it.
**Pam** It was Daddy's middle name.
**Frank** I know.
**Pam** Oh well. We'll stick to Bobby, then, shall we?
**Frank** He'll adjust. Ms Vincent said they usually do.

*The Lights fade*

*When the Lights come up Miss Bradfield is seated*

*Frank and Pam stand and listen*

**Bradfield** Oh certainly, certainly. He's done remarkably well. Considering his late start.
**Pam** There you are, Frank. I told you.
**Bradfield** Yes. We're delighted. Very pleased indeed. On the whole.
**Pam** Frank and I have been wondering about options, Miss Bradfield.

**Bradfield** Options?
**Frank** Yes. We ought to start structuring his career.
**Bradfield** I see...
**Frank** I'm talking about exams, Miss Bradfield.
**Bradfield** I realize that but he's still in top infants and top infants don't do exams.
**Pam** But he's been tested...
**Bradfield** Of course.
**Pam** Well, tests are exams, aren't they?
**Bradfield** Not in the sense that I think you mean. They won't give him anything he can use to gain a place in further education, for example. The leap from top infants to Sixth Form College is rather a large one. Even for a rabbit.
**Frank** But we can't leave it too long, can we? I mean, if we're not careful he'll be drawing a pension before he's out of short trousers.
**Bradfield** Pension?
**Frank** In a manner of speaking.
**Pam** He doesn't wear trousers, Frank.
**Bradfield** I'm afraid pensions don't come under our umbrella at all, Mr Gideon.
**Frank** No, of course. I wasn't being serious.
**Pam** I thought we agreed that trousers would be humiliating...
**Frank** It was a joke, Mother.
**Bradfield** As a matter of fact, the tests you're speaking of have revealed one or two hiccups as far as Bobby's progress is concerned.
**Frank** Hiccups?
**Bradfield** Yes. His reading appears to be well above average for a child of his age. He loves books. Devours them. Sometimes literally, in fact. But there are some gaps in other areas of the curriculum. His handwriting, for instance.
**Pam** What's wrong with his handwriting?

**Bradfield** He doesn't join his letters in the accepted fashion, Mrs Gideon.
**Frank** That's because he doesn't do it like the other children do.
**Bradfield** Meaning?
**Frank** Well, he holds the pencil in his mouth. So you can't actually call it *hand*writing, can you?
**Bradfield** It doesn't matter what I call it. The National Curriculum calls it handwriting.
**Frank** Didn't I tell you, Mother? We've been too soft on him...
**Bradfield** There's also science. He hasn't yet managed to carry out the simplest experiments the other children take in their stride.
**Pam** Well, he can't hold the equipment.
**Bradfield** And technology.
**Frank** Technology? I thought you said you were pleased with him.
**Bradfield** We are. He's done well. We just need to iron out these wrinkles. Like technology. You see, he hasn't actually made anything that could be assessed yet.
**Frank** Well, as Mother says...
**Bradfield** I know. He can't hold the equipment. The trouble is that at his age he should be holding the equipment. At the very least. There are also some gaps in his oral profile.
**Frank** His what?
**Bradfield** Asking and answering questions. At the most basic level. Giving directions. Taking messages home.
**Pam** He does bring messages home.
**Bradfield** Yes but I have to write them down and put them in his lunch box.
**Frank** What's wrong with that? It seems to work.
**Bradfield** If I had to do that for all the children I'd be so busy writing notes that the National Curriculum would more or less fly out of the window.

**Pam** Well, Bobby can't help that. He can't speak, Miss Bradfield.

**Bradfield** Quite. This is exactly what his oral profile has unearthed. An interviewer might deem that kind of thing dumb insolence.

**Frank** I see. Has he been playing up, then?

**Bradfield** Well, at times he does seem rather sullen.

**Pam** How can you tell he's sullen? He doesn't speak.

**Bradfield** That's what being sullen is, Mrs Gideon.

**Frank** Surely it's more than just that...

**Bradfield** It is exactly that.

**Frank** But...

**Bradfield** The local authority, in response to pressure from various parent bodies, has produced a working paper on common disruptive behaviour. And I ought to know because I was on the working party working on the working paper. I quote. "The sullen child is the child who refuses to communicate his wishes or to respond to the wishes of others. In extreme cases, the sullen child opts for complete silence." That, officially, is what sullenness is.

**Pam** But if someone can't speak at all, how do you know when they're *choosing* not to speak?

**Bradfield** I told you. I was on the working party.

**Pam** Yes but...

**Bradfield** I'm sorry, Mrs Gideon. I have nothing more to say on the matter.

**Frank** I see. (*Beat*) But basically you're pleased with Bobby?

**Bradfield** Up to a point. In certain areas.

**Frank** But in other areas...?

**Bradfield** He's lagging.

**Frank** Can't he be given extra help or something?

**Bradfield** He is being given help. That's what I'm doing here in my lunch-break. Helping.

**Frank** I mean in the class. Can't he have someone to watch over

him and pass his notes to you?
**Bradfield** You mean ancillary help?
**Frank** If that's what it's called, yes.
**Bradfield** No, he can't. To be given that kind of favoured treatment Bobby would have to be classified as a Special Needs child.
**Pam** Well, he's a rabbit. That's fairly special.
**Bradfield** Not special in the agreed sense. There has to be an official statement to the effect that he's special.
**Frank** That's the answer, then, isn't it?
**Bradfield** What?
**Frank** Get this statement which says that Bobby has these special needs and then he can have some help.
**Bradfield** No.
**Pam** Why not?
**Bradfield** Because he still has a reading age above his chronological age. And that means he does not have special needs. Not the sort that require notes being written for him.
**Pam** How does all this fit in with his options, then?
**Bradfield** It's all fairly germane actually.
**Pam** Is it?
**Bradfield** Yes. Effectively, taking the whole of his profile and the test results into consideration...
**Frank** He hasn't got any. Options, I mean.
**Bradfield** I wouldn't go that far.
**Frank** But he'll have to stay in your class?
**Bradfield** Well...
**Pam** What?
**Bradfield** There is another course of action available to us.
**Frank** What is it?
**Bradfield** (*beat*) We're thinking of moving him in with Miss O'Connor.
**Frank** Miss O'Connor? That's middle infants, isn't it?

**Bradfield** Yes.

**Pam** Move him down, you mean?

**Bradfield** I mean find him a more suitable placement.

**Frank** Demote him.

**Bradfield** It would make sense. Apart from anything else, Mr Hendry has had complaints about Bobby.

**Pam** What sort of complaints?

**Bradfield** Representations from the PTA. (*Checking her clipboard*) One mother says Bobby is allowed to get away without doing PE...

**Frank** Is that all?

**Bradfield** There's also been a bit of an incident. You see, some of Bobby's chums took him out of his cage. Next door. To say hallo to the other rabbit.

**Frank** To Fluff?

**Pam** What's wrong with that?

**Bradfield** Nothing. It would've been a harmless jape. If Bobby had stopped at hallo.

**Frank** Oh dear...

**Pam** You mean...

**Bradfield** Yes. It's given Mr Hendry something of a disciplinary tangle to unravel. You see, whilst Bobby's actions are not against school rules *per se*, they don't set a very good example to the other children. And they may, of course, have repercussions in the not too distant future.

**Pam** Babies.

**Frank** Oh dear...

**Bradfield** Which throws up a whole new set of difficulties.

**Pam** You mean, will the babies be able to read and write?

**Bradfield** Indeed. And what is Bobby's status as parent *and* pupil in the same infant department? All these things are going to put a strain on the legal chappies in the office.

**Frank** So you're moving him to Miss O'Connor's?

**Bradfield**  For a start, yes. To see if he can pull his socks up.
**Pam**  And if he can't?
**Bradfield**  If he can't we have to ask ourselves whether school is the right place for him.
**Frank**  But where else could he go?
**Bradfield**  (*beat*) We've been thinking of some sort of research posting...
**Frank**  Research? But he won't have the qualifications.
**Bradfield**  He won't need qualifications.
**Frank**  Sort of Youth Training Scheme?
**Bradfield**  Yes, I suppose so.
**Pam**  In what field?
**Bradfield**  Science.
**Frank**  A laboratory?
**Pam**  But, Miss Bradfield, I've already explained. He couldn't hold the equipment.
**Bradfield**  He won't need to hold the equipment, Mrs Gideon.

*Frank and Pam look at each other, realizing what this means*

But that's some way off. Let's hope he makes more of an effort to conform to what's already being provided for him, shall we?

*They all peer into the cage as it begins to judder again*

*The Lights fade as Miss Bradfield smiles and leaves*

*The Lights come up to find Frank standing by the cage reading a note. Pam is reading her book. She looks up suddenly*

**Pam**  Frank?
**Frank**  Hmm?
**Pam**  What's up?

**Frank** (*sitting down*) Nothing.
**Pam** What have you got there?
**Frank** Nothing.
**Pam** You have. It's another note, isn't it?
**Frank** Yes. It doesn't amount to much, though.
**Pam** What does it say?
**Frank** Well, you know Bobby...
**Pam** Frank.

*Frank passes Pam the note*

**Frank** I don't think he means it. It's a kind of joke.
**Pam** P-i-s... Oh, Frank. Where does he pick up language like this?
**Frank** Not from me, if that's what you're suggesting.
**Pam** Of course not. It must be the school. It must be the middle infants.
**Frank** It's unnerving somehow, isn't it?
**Pam** It's unnerving all right.
**Frank** I mean, he's only used one "s" and one "f". He's never got the hang of double letters. Not even in his own name.
**Pam** I don't think he sees the point. And, anyway, it's not the spelling that unnerves me. It's the sentiment.
**Frank** Quite.
**Pam** Do you think he means us? Is that what he wants us to do, Frank?
**Frank** Maybe. Or maybe he means Ms Vincent.
**Pam** Or Mr Hendry, or Miss O'Connor.
**Frank** Maybe he means the whole lot of us.
**Pam** Yes, well. I wouldn't blame him if he did.
**Frank** I know what you mean, but couched in these terms...
**Pam** It's what I think sometimes.
**Frank** What, these particular words?

**Pam** Very nearly.

**Frank** Well, I wouldn't want to hear you say it, Mother. Much as I might agree with... Oh no!

**Pam** What? What is it?

**Frank** I've left the door open, look.

**Pam** Oh, Frank.

**Frank** It must've been open for five minutes or more.

*He gets up to close it*

**Pam** No, Frank. Wait.

**Frank** What?

**Pam** Just leave it a moment.

**Frank** What? He'll get out.

**Pam** He might, I suppose.

**Frank** Yes, but Mother...

**Pam** What if he does? Would that be such a terrible thing?

**Frank** Yes. Yes it would. We'd have Ms Vincent on our backs for a start. Closely followed by the PTA, the Governors, the head...

**Pam** But what about Bobby?

**Frank** Well exactly. We're responsible for him.

**Pam** I know, I know.

**Frank** And what would Mr Lennox say if he ever heard?

**Pam** It's got nothing to do with Mr Lennox.

**Frank** I'm not saying it has, but he still might hear about it, Mother. And then what, eh?

**Pam** Calm down, Frank.

**Frank** Calm down?

**Pam** Listen, you're always so careful with that door. With everything to do with Bobby. You never make mistakes...

**Frank** Until now.

**Pam** No, Frank. Be honest with yourself. Not even now.

**Frank** What are you getting at?
**Pam** That door was no accident, was it?
**Frank** Of course it was...
**Pam** Subconsciously it wasn't, I mean.
**Frank** (*sitting*) Well... I don't know.
**Pam** Bobby's not a fool, in spite of what Miss Bradfield might say. Maybe we should...
**Frank** Let him go?
**Pam** Maybe we should. Maybe that's what you meant by leaving the door open.
**Frank** But he's got a Technology test on Thursday...
**Pam** So what? By Thursday, Frank, he could be in the country. Miles away from any Technology tests.
**Frank** We'd have Ms Vincent to face, though.
**Pam** I don't care. To be honest, I think she's a bit of a berk...
**Frank** Mother.
**Pam** Well. What with her suits and clipboards and not knowing tea from a bag when it's under her nose.

*Pause*

**Frank** Set him free, you mean?
**Pam** Why not? Let him make up his own mind what he wants.

*They turn and look at the cage*

Bobby! Are you awake in there?
**Frank** Bobby. We're not going to force you or anything but... (*To Pam*) He hasn't moved.
**Pam** It's the jump, Frank. He's too high off the ground.
**Frank** Right.

*They gather cushions and place them against the cage. As they do* so...

**Pam** You can decide for yourself, Bobby...
**Frank** You're quite old enough...
**Pam** Don't worry about us...
**Frank** You do what's best. We'll be all right...
**Pam** There's fields and grass and what have you...
**Frank** It's up to you now, Bobby.

*They return to their chairs. Slight juddering sounds. Bobby is certainly in there*

We could get something else. A kitten or something.
**Pam** A kitten, Frank?
**Frank** If you like.
**Pam** Daddy couldn't abide cats. You know that.
**Frank** That's settled, then. A cat. A big ginger tom that'll spray all over his rock garden.
**Pam** (*laughing*) Oh, how awful.
**Frank** What do you say, then?
**Pam** Oh no. I don't think so. Not after Bobby. But thank you very much.
**Frank** Well. We'll see. (*Pause*) Bobby!
**Pam** We won't look. If that makes you feel better.

*They turn the chairs round. The Lights fade, leaving a spot on the cage*

**Frank** It's up to you, Bobby.
**Pam** Bobby?

*Darkness now but for the light on the cage. There are sounds of movement. The Light fades. Music*

# FURNITURE AND PROPERTY LIST

*On stage*: Rabbit cage containing newspaper and pencil
Chairs with cushions
Books
Newspaper
Cup of tea
Box. *In it*: simple books and alaphabet charts
Pieces of paper

*Off stage*: Tray of tea things (**Pam**)

*Personal*: **Bradfield**: clipboard

## LIGHTING PLOT

Property fittings required: nil
Interior. The same throughout

*To open*: darkness

Cue 1   When ready (Page 1)
*Bring up general lighting*

Cue 2   **Frank:** "... looking pleased with himself." (Page 7)
*Lights fade*

Cue 3   When ready (Page 7)
*Bring up general lighting*

Cue 4   **Vincent:** "... see how he gets on." (Page 12)
*Fade lights*

Cue 5   When ready (Page 13)
*Bring up general lighting*

Cue 6   **Frank:** "... they usually do." (Page 25)
*Fade lights*

Cue 7   When ready (Page 25)
*Bring up general lighting*

Cue 8   **Miss Bradfield** smiles and leaves (Page 31)
*Fade lights*

*Cue* 9  When ready (Page 31)
  *Bring up lights*

*Cue* 10 They turn the chairs round (Page 35)
  *Fade lights, leaving spot on cage*

*Cue* 11 Sounds of movement (Page 35)
  *Lights fade*

# EFFECTS PLOT

*Cue* 1 Sounds of movement from cage  (Page 1)

*Cue* 2 **Frank:** "... message anyway."  (Page 14)
*Doorbell*

*Cue* 3 **Pam:** "... be best."  (Page 14)
*Doorbell*

*Cue* 4 **Frank:** "... ashamed of them."  (Page 24)
*Thumping from within cage*

*Cue* 5 They all peer into the cage  (Page 31)
*Sounds of movement from cage*

*Cue* 6 They return to their chairs  (Page 35)
*Slight juddering from cage*

*Cue* 7 Spot on cage  (Page 35)
*Sounds of movement from cage.*
*Music*

www.ingramcontent.com/pod-product-compliance
Lightning Source LLC
Chambersburg PA
CBHW070453050426
42450CB00012B/3255